Scarlet Rain Boots

poems by

Mary Salisbury

Finishing Line Press
Georgetown, Kentucky

Scarlet Rain Boots

*To my husband, Bob "Slats" Salisbury,
my life long companion and friend,
who encouraged me with his good humor,
and loved me as I am.*

Copyright © 2020 by Mary Salisbury
ISBN 978-1-64662-206-1 First Edition
All rights reserved under International and Pan-American Copyright Conventions.
No part of this book may be reproduced in any manner whatsoever without written permission from the publisher, except in the case of brief quotations embodied in critical articles and reviews.

Publisher: Leah Maines
Editor: Christen Kincaid
Cover Art: Bob Salisbury
Author Photo: Emily Salisbury
Cover Design: Elizabeth Maines McCleavy

Printed in the USA on acid-free paper.
Order online: www.finishinglinepress.com
       also available on amazon.com

         Author inquiries and mail orders:
              Finishing Line Press
                P. O. Box 1626
          Georgetown, Kentucky 40324
                   U. S. A.

Table of Contents

Welsh Mare 1
Reckless 3
Our Daily Bread 4
Notes 5
In Kitchens 6
Breaking Bread 7
Don't Look Back 8
Dark Blue Boat 9
The Banks of the Loire 10
Afterwards 11
Tanager 12
Ribbons Flying 13
Notes on Aspens 14
After You Left 15
Night 16
Hopping on One Leg 17
Tussled 18
Her Body 19
August in Portland 20
Long Gone 21
Mutual Friend 22
Listen Anyway 23
Nature 24
Triumphant 25
Kicking at the Gate 26
Sterling Creek 27
Plenty 28
Ripening 29
Anew 30
Each Leaf 31
Corralled 32

Everyone can master a grief but he that has it.

—*William Shakespeare*

Welsh Mare

She carried our children up meadow,
meeting dusty roads.
Heading home, the leafy stretch,
the dip in darkness
where the tunnel of trees
thickens, near the wild oak.
Now her gray-flecked body thins, grazing
the open meadow, she makes
the graceful leap over the spring fed creek.
When she naps, front and back legs each atop the other,
on her side facing away,
there's no coaxing her to rise up running.

The snow crusted hard over everything
and her whinny-call long and demanding,
her feet stomping on the wooden gate,
her breath in white puffs, fur frosted,
catching the slanting lines of light
where today, the first signs of thaw peek
from the faded winter grass.
She could take a spill, break something,
after all the bending to bridles
she's come to this: confined to shelter,
fed flakes of light green hay and apples.
Orchards she once walked through:
Prima, Winesap, Arkansas Black.

Today you feed her oats off the front porch,
her fur thick and stiff, white with frost,
age thirty-four, two days before Christmas.
You go inside to fetch warm water,
stainless steel bowl steaming
when it meets the cold air.
The mare licks each oat,
stares at the water, her hooves long and rough.
On the side porch a box of apples,
Jonathans from the tree out back,
tough waxy skin, a red deep and bewildering,
wrapping the fruit like clotted blood.
A neighbor's gun sounds in the distance.
You and the mare look up.

Reckless

Remember the garden swing,
how she couldn't get enough of you?
The glory of oblivion, kissing her:
robin, lilac, grape hyacinth,
the emerald grass. She, twining
flowers in your buttonhole.
You arrived full of yesterday,
She was already late.
You carried letters from a dead woman,
She was halfway out the gate.
It has always been this way with you,
scattered petals on your path.
Fanciful and reckless,
foraged ancient maps.
Light like crushed wax paper.
Piles of hay in random rows.
Don't look back.

Our Daily Bread

Was that it?
What just went by.
Was that our life?
The pale blue sky.
The songs of love,
our dancing feet,
The urgent path,
ascent to peace.
The children we were,
the ones we had.
The prayers we said,
our daily bread.
Was lightning quick,
and graceful slow,
this reckoning
to getting old.

Notes

You waited till the bells were ringing.
Sat among the mournful singing.
Polished anguish into joy.
Let the music fill your soul.
Offered up your leaden pulse.
Kept your head but not your heart.

In Kitchens

Remember how the steam rose,
from inside the deep wide pan?
You waiting, tongue curling,
briskly wiping hands,
one-two, your blue apron.
Sliding the sticky noodles free,
tumbling under the cool water.
The handful from colander to plate.
Two meatballs to top it off.
Tablespoons of Parmesan.
Your mouth opening wide.

Breaking Bread

Many meals came and went
and years of sunlit days.
The grass greened, snow fell,
you never came to stay.
Many nights, slivers of moon,
and mornings soft with rain.
The seasons stirred, then turned,
you never came to stay.

Don't Look Back

You coming to her
like showers of gold
filtering through
the weakened roof.
Though she bore you
no children, old beyond
the bearing of life,
you, beyond the slaying
of others, adrift in
your own locked vessel,
under the Hunter's moon,
on your own lost sea.

A Dark Blue Boat

There was a dark blue boat
they were planning to sail,
even dreamed a future,
before they knew about
not making plans.
Dark blue with red trim,
behind the shed.
When everything went
up in smoke they lost
the dark blue boat.

The Banks of the Loire

Luminous light,
the golden liquid day.
Laughter stretching
beyond damp cellars,
where bottles turned
in the cool, moist earth.
Lie down along
the sunny bank
of the Loire.
Shake the cloth,
drape the linen down.
Take the day back.

Afterwards

Every morning you walk the narrow path,
birdsong flying furiously.
You with the Tanager, Robin, Oriole.
Their feathers bright and orange.
The gathered cosmos violet,
your hands full of flowers.

Tanager

Last night a Western Tanager flew into the window,
tremors of orange and yellow skirted the balcony.
A half hour went by.
When you looked it was gone to the dusk
of swooping swallows and bats,
the mad maze of newly leafed oak,
the swift ungoverned night.

Ribbons Flying

He eclipsed everything.
There was salvation in surrender,
the wound of animal magnetism.
Time rendered the new less potent,
an ancient story.
He never meant to be heartless.
She sensed the sleeping dogs,
chained to a nearby bike stand,
a park bench as far away
as the Tuileries.
No one gets off scot-free.
The widening day, layers
like ash settling on what was.
She clung to the invisible
flying ribbons.

Notes on Aspens

Five pencil thin aspens,
dancing silhouettes
on the beige building.
Their pale silver bark
spreading shadows,
a row of symmetry,
a beauty brilliant enough
to awaken desire.

After You Left

A ruinous gray covered the car.
A late night storm taking trees down.
A Doug fir blocked the driveway,
a welcome barricade.
Rain pelted the windshield
like the steady beat of drums.
Mud oozing, puddles becoming pond.
Snow, once safe in shade, melting
into runoff, as sorrow spread to earth,
its ragged melancholy cloak.

Night

Beyond the age the young imagine,
leaves rustling beneath us.
Down the street children jump rope,
a lone streetlight elongates shadows.
Wild time slipping away.
We willfully take stores to last
through the coming winter.

Hopping on One Leg

The robin dances on the green grass,
May shade dappling the hydrangea,
the swing facing the ravine and creek.
The robin flashing dusty orange,
hopping on one-leg.
The man and woman
absorb the art of diffusion,
letting secrets pass.
Their feet, the steaming ground,
the steady repetition of birdsong:
come home, come home.

Tussled

At a crossroads, turn right.
No need to keep turning left.
The world of the two of you
excluded everybody else.
This was your undoing.
A world as primitive
and passing never had
the chance of lasting.
Tussled like seed,
until a cloudburst
pummeled you both back
to the leveling ground.
A field of mustard,
waves of lavender.
Inside the wildness
you never stood a chance.

Her Body

Her body knows things, the knowing
deepest where life takes shape,
a sea away, elsewhere.
Furrowed seeds yield golden life.
Monument maker, woman,
bearer of bodies and souls.
A history of humans, her blood
forever mixing, her steps the steps
they took, passengers alive and light
as honeycombs, rich with promise.
Women carry, etching marks in catacombs.
No oracle has solved the riddle yet.
Beyond sunset, she carries history.

August in Portland

Words said low, short blasts of heat
five decades in the making. We took
the path by the wide Willamette,
aspen trees guiding the way,
absorbing our blows.
The back and forth of chance.
All our old passions,
the ancient rivalry.
We sat outside on the grassy verge,
downing Dewar's and Grey Goose.
Pleasure boats and a string of kayaks
in dusky silhouette skimming to shore.
A lone canoe threading silver ripples,
bobbing waves, the liquid glimmering.
We, in iron chairs pulled close to the
iron table, the smell of good fish nearby.
We order another round, our tongues
thickening, the wounding cast to sea.

Long Gone

The brown November leaves drop,
one and then another, this windless day,
one week before Thanksgiving.
As if there's all the time in the world
for letting you go, for leaves
and trees and windless days.
All the leaves now brown,
the red and yellow, the orange,
the green, long gone.

Mutual Friend

Charles Dickens is dead.
We wait in doctor's rooms,
magazines dated years ago.
We wait, you and me
and Little Nell.
Books from the library,
filled with friends;
some of them dead.
It may be one-sided.
We'll never know if
the feeling is mutual.
O make me laugh again,
take me with you
my dear old friend.

Listen Anyway

Chances are someone
tells you your life
won't be the same.

Maybe it happens
before Christmas,
everyone festive,
except those who lean
toward depression.

You pack boxes,
dismantling your life.
Chances are you move
without direction.
Your fate like footsteps
in the snow.

Nature

There was some heat
still shimmering between them
despite the stacking of years.
He felt it too, she could tell,
the way a horse flicks its tail
to swat flies.

Triumphant

A refugee seeks peace.
Centuries knocking,
a chanting mob
of history.
The face
of nobility.
Ave Maria.
Welcome the bones,
O ancient border.
History deep in body,
coming home.
A song triumphant,
haunting to shore.

Kicking at the Gate

You won't know it's the last time.
A picnic by the Applegate river,
the drive up to Lake of the Woods.
Sleeping in your house, the one
you built, laying gray foundation
blocks, framing walls, a friend who
helped you build the stairs.

You won't know it's the last time
walking out to the barn,
grain in hand, where the horse
waits, kicking at the gate.

You take the same walk later,
the mare down now,
breathing hard, legs too weak
to stand, and you know
this is the last time.

You fill U-Haul boxes,
Stack them in empty rooms,
Your echoing footsteps
a flicker of what might
rain down, a thunderclap.

Maybe it's best not to know.
The blue door shutting,
the yellow farmhouse pulsing
in the morning sun.
The meadow still, a few deer
working on the grass.

Sterling Creek

You swim.
Backstroke is best.
Eyes closed, float.
Half circle, turn.
Repeat.
What do you have
to lose?

Sterling Creek,
gliding down Woodrat,
the sweet yellow house.
Madrone, Manzanita,
Mountain lilac. Juniper.

Field grass blowing,
deer in bouncing flight,
white tails bobbing,
the coyote calls at night.
You did your best.
It could have gone
the other way.

Popcorn flowers,
ladder by the apple tree.
The aspen beside the house
to remind you of Colorado,
leaves like ancient coins,
spinning in October.

Plenty

Clouds of sparrow swoop the stalks,
greed-eating corn seed.
Nearby, an orchard of pears,
ornaments of bronze and yellow.
This land of plenty.
Hay, cut and stacked,
three-sided barns filled.
Rows of squash, like skulls,
pale on the frozen fields.
Expect the clouds to part.
This land of plenty.
Blackbirds aloft,
biding their time.
You singing Bobby McGee,
nights coming early and cold,
the world's on fire.

Ripening

Pears dazzling in September,
trace of golden blush,
soon to swoon to ground.
A deer tilting its head up
to catch the juice and feast
until the shriek of turkeys
descend, devouring.

Anew

Blue, the shade,
a robin's egg,
the bird emerges,
a song, a rush of notes.
Butterflies on leaves,
Ladybugs sunning,
foxglove petals slipping,
green, the lawn.
Swimming, she rises,
breaking the surface,
her deep breaths,
the world fresh as death.

Each Leaf

O the stories we told as the years went by,
the red, the gold, the red, the gold, the green.
We loved and laughed and lived in the between.
The green goes and the yellow goes,
And the red will soon be gone.
These colors couldn't last.
Each tree stripped bare, wind fierce and chill,
by morning leaves will be everywhere.
Watching the color fade from your face
left me longing for things we hadn't done.
It seems I've spent a lifetime staring
at the red vine covering the side of this building.
Each streak of sunlight lengthening to shadow.
The red, the gold, the red, the gold, the green.
The wind blows. The red and yellow leaves
are falling. You say you want to listen to music.
A spell to be spun by the sound of memory.
O Eternity.
Each breath I watch you take a reminder:
We are as separate as the leaves.
And the green goes,
And the gold goes.
There is a window, steel sun,
cranes of light, a river,
there is the sunny clamor of the living.
The red, the gold, the red, the gold, the green.
Last night you took one nap after another.

Corralled

She has come to this—confined to shelter.
Clouds form fists of charcoal,
January gray,
her whinny not like before.
The vet wore scarlet rain boots.
And you remembered the narrow lanes
of Ireland, shade and green,
Fuchsia archways, and a banshee cry
in your bones, deep as ancestors.
Now it was just the memory of sound,
the mare's head in your lap,
your knees slick with mud.
You didn't wear the right shoes.
The silver needle promises
its own kind of peace.
A bright blue tarp to wrap her in,
the dark earth mounting beside us
as the backhoe claws rise and fall.
We roll her into the grave,
there, in the field behind the barn.
Our yellow lab pees on the spot:
dog version of holy water.
Your beloved rakes the loose clay,
a bed of grief,
reminding us of what's ahead.

Mary Salisbury's poetry has appeared in *Calyx*, and her first chapbook, *Come What May*, was published by Finishing Line Press. The poem, "Welsh Mare Corralled," was a finalist for the Orlando Poetry Prize. Mary's short fiction has been published in Cutthroat's *Truth to Power*. Salisbury was awarded Honorable Mention with Glimmer Train twice and named a finalist twice for the Rick DeMarinis story award. *Fiction Southeast* published an essay by Mary in their "Why I Write" column. An Oregon Literary Arts Fellowship recipient, and a graduate of Pacific University's MFA in writing, Mary Salisbury lives outside of Portland, Oregon.

www.ingramcontent.com/pod-product-compliance
Lightning Source LLC
LaVergne TN
LVHW040117080426
835507LV00041B/1281